Introducing Handbuilt Pottery

WITHDRAWN

1 Diameters approximately 127 mm (5 in.)
Seed case forms pinched up from discs of
very thin clay. Glazed in white with red iron
oxide stippled on to the edges with a sponge

© Tony Jolly 1973
First published in Great Britain 1973
ISBN 0 7134 2443 5
First published in the United States 1974
by Watson-Guptill Publications,
a division of Billboard Publications, Inc.

Library of Congress Cataloging in Publication Data
Bibliography: p.
1. Pottery craft. I. Title.
TT920.J64 1974   738.1   73-8877
ISBN 0-8230-6194-9
Made and printed in Great Britain by
William Clowes and Sons Ltd
Beccles, Suffolk
for the publishers
B. T. Batsford Limited
4 Fitzhardinge Street, London W1H 0AH
and Watson-Guptill Publications
One Astor Plaza, New York, N.Y. 10036

Jacket photographs by Tony Lindford

2 Height 470 mm (18½ in.)
Slab construction with upper and lower parts
built and fired separately, and finally joined
with glue

Introducing Handbuilt Pottery

Tony Jolly

B. T. Batsford Limited London
Watson-Guptill Publications New York

3 Height 292 mm (11½ in.)
   Sand casting in which a slip of coarse,
   grogged, clay was poured into depressions
   formed in damp sand with pieces of wood.
   The cast is coated with several colours of
   glaze, each applied by slip trailer

Contents

Acknowledgement

I wish to thank Mary, my wife, for her great patience and assistance in the preparation of material for the book, Ruth Gilbert for her interest, advice and kiln facilities, Mary Hedges for her work in typing out the manuscript, and Tony Lindford for his invaluable work in processing my photographs and preparing the finished prints.

4 *Height 203 mm (8 in.)*
Slab built architectural construction in coarse clay, partly glazed in white and with green bottle-glass fired into the recesses

Introduction

The histories of cultures and civilisations over several millenia are recorded in their pottery. Clay has played an important part in the life of man from the early times in which he used clay in its unfired state in the form of building materials, domestic wares, or votive objects. The history of pottery began with the possibly accidental discovery that the hitherto fragile clay could be transformed by fire into something that was hard and durable. Whilst many other materials have disintegrated with the passing of time, fired clay remains almost unmarked. Museums across the world display the multitude of responses which man has made to this most basic of materials.

In the industrialized countries, pottery production has long ceased to be a local craft although the old traditions survive in many other parts of the world. At the same time as the pottery industry is becoming even more mechanized there is a growing interest in craft pottery, and many firms, especially in Scandinavia, provide individual potters with lavish facilities in return for ideas which can be developed for commercial production. This interest is shared by children and adults who take an active part in the craft as well as by those who buy the potters' work simply for the pleasure it gives.

Just as attitudes to materials and techniques in painting and sculpture have changed, so the art of the potter is undergoing a similar revision. Clay is no longer regarded as a material to be formed solely into domestic ware and there is now a much wider appreciation of the unique properties it possesses as a medium for a personal interpretation and understanding of the environment. This book is intended to show a little of the latent qualities of clay in handbuilt forms and to stimulate a desire to use the material in a free way.

5 *Height 229 mm (9 in.)*
   Basically a cylinder of clay to which coils
   were added for legs, neck, head and rider with
   some carving at the leather-hard stage.
   Painted decoration in red iron oxide, yellow
   ochre stain, gum and water, applied directly to
   the biscuit-fired piece. Unglazed. Modelled
   after studies of painted Cypriot ware c 1100 BC

Equipment

Kilns

Kilns can be fired by electricity, gas, oil, wood, or solid fuels: all reference to kiln operation in this book concern electricity. Electric kilns are relatively inexpensive to purchase and operate, easy to maintain, and simple to fire. The heating is by elements set in the fire brick lined walls of the kiln (see figure 112). Elements do age and ultimately fail but when carefully used and maintained last for a long time. Keep a stock of replacement elements and seek expert instruction on their installation. If possible, the minimum size of the firing chamber should be 381 mm × 381 mm × 508 mm (15 in. × 15 in. × 20 in.) and the kiln should be capable of operation to 1300°C. Even though this level may not be needed initially, it will be necessary when stoneware clay is used. The interior should be kept clean of firing dust and debris, especially in the element channels, and a suction cleaner is ideal for the purpose.

Shelving, shelf props and pot stilts are supplied in a variety of temperature grades and those purchased should be capable of withstanding the maximum firing temperature of the kiln. New shelves should be treated with a wash made from equal parts of china clay and flint with enough water to mix up to paint consistency. The coating protects the shelves from glaze runs or drips during the glost firing and should be renewed as necessary. Glaze marks on the shelves should be thoroughly covered and glaze runs chipped away with a cold chisel, immersing the shelf in water to prevent flying glaze splinters. Keep a table or shelf near the kiln on which to store the kiln furniture and to stand pots whilst packing the kiln.

Work bench

This should be strongly made with a solid working surface set at a height comfortable for working standing or seated on a stool. The top is best in timber but a bench of poured concrete slabs set on stone or brick piers gives a solid and inexpensive working surface. Wedging clay imposes great strains on the workbench and will soon batter a flimsy structure to pieces.

Sink and water supply

A water supply is essential, as is a sink large enough to hold the bowls and buckets in use in the pottery. Silting clay and plaster waste can block drains, so care must be taken to allow the minimum of each to be washed away on cleaning equipment in the sink.

Shelving and storage

Adequate shelving space is needed for the storage of work, equipment and materials. Cupboards for storing bisque ware and a damp cupboard (one with water trays in the base) for greenware under construction are desirable but not essential; polythene or polyethylene sheeting is an adequate substitute.

Containers

Lidded galvanized or plastic containers are needed for clay storage, one for each type of clay in use, and others for the reclamation of waste clay. Plastic buckets with tightly fitting lids are required for slips and glazes, and plastic bowls, jugs and buckets are useful in many situations. Some containers may be improvised, and so cost nothing; glass jars with screw top lids are ideal for storing chemicals purchased in small quantities or drawn from bulk stock. Materials bought in bulk can be kept in the supplier's packaging. Remember to clearly and securely label all containers and packages.

Organisation and safety

Careful organization of the work space, materials and equipment is important, especially when several people are to use the pottery. Storage space for tools and small equipment should be clearly defined, even labelled, and all containers for raw materials, slips, glazes etc. should be boldly marked as to contents. A routine should be established which allows the easy organization of glaze mixing, clay reclamation and kiln firings, whilst leaving the maximum amount of time available for making pots. The pottery should be kept tidy and reasonably clean.

Some safety precautions must be observed, particularly in the operation of the kiln which should be padlocked and carry a prominent warning during the whole firing cycle. Ventilation should be provided to clear dampness or the hot dry air associated with a firing. Dust should be kept to a minimum as some of the dry materials are extremely abrasive and slip or glaze materials should only be mixed together after water has been added to them. Heavy weights should be lifted carefully and shelving kept to a height which can be reached without undue stretching. A fire extinguisher and asbestos fire blanket should be maintained and basic fire precautions observed.

Temperature chart

Centigrade	Fahrenheit
0	32
20	68
30	86
50	122
100	212
200	392
250	482
300	572
350	662
500	932
550	1022
600	1112
1000	1832
1100	2012
1200	2192
1300	2372
1400	2552
1500	2732

The above are equivalents for all temperature instructions mentioned in the text.

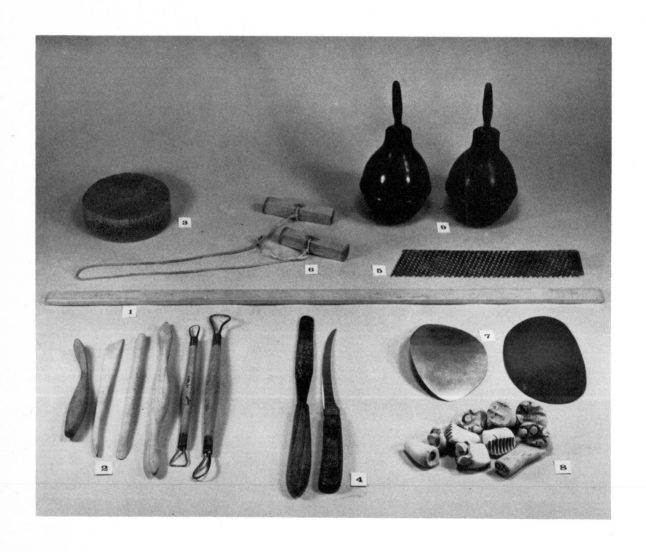

6 *A selection of hand tools*

Hand tools

A variety of hand tools is needed, some of which can be adapted from scrap materials, whilst others are obtained from the local ironmonger or from the pottery supplier. Tools in common use are illustrated in figure (6) and detailed below.

1 Straight edge

These are best in metal but hardwood is quite adequate until it begins to warp; one straight edge should be marked as a ruler.

2 Modelling tools

Those illustrated are of boxwood, some being fitted with wire loop ends: equally adptable tools can be whittled from scrap hardwood.

3 Sponges

Large synthetic sponges are suitable for wiping up benches and bowls whilst the smaller sizes, or natural sponges, are used in making pottery.

4 Knives

A broad bladed artist's palette knife is extremely useful for fine cutting but kitchen and table knives are ideal as general purpose cutters. A sharp craft knife is useful for piercing through leather hard pieces.

5 Planer files ('Surform' two-way tool)

These are intended for use with wood but are excellent for finishing work: handles are not essential.

6 Wedging wire

The handles are of scrap wood drilled to take a length of strong nylon fishing line, metal wire or string.

7 Kidneys (Finishing Rubbers)

These are of rubber or metal and are available in a range of sizes and curvatures: metal versions can easily be cut from food cans and their edges filed. Kidneys are used for shaping or scraping the insides of curved forms.

8 Stamps

Stamps of biscuit fired clay, plaster or found objects are kept for use in texturing clay surfaces.

9 Slip trailers

Used in slipware. The trailers are usually of rubber or polythene with plug-in nozzles.

Clays

Types and selection

Clay is available in plastic form ready for use, the principal types being earthenware and stoneware. Most suppliers offer a variety of blends which have their own particular working properties, texture, and fired colour. Earthenwares can be white, buff, and brown, while stonewares range from almost white to a deep brownish-black. Earthenware is glost fired at approximately 1100°C and stoneware in excess of 1200°C; suppliers always state the firing temperatures for each of their clays. Stoneware is hard and durable as well as being impervious to water, whereas earthenware is much softer and porous. In glaze colouring earthenware has the advantage when brilliance of colour is looked for but stoneware glazes have a richness and subtlety entirely their own. Earthenware is ideal for modelling and for use in traditional English slipware.

When deciding on the clay to be purchased remember that each type will require its own storage facilities and glaze ranges and that, although the two can be mixed in biscuit firings, they must be glazed separately. In practice this is not a serious difficulty.

Do not neglect local clays which can give considerable interest through the sequence of digging, cleaning and experimental firing. A satisfactory local clay will also provide a cheap supply of a basic raw material. Local brickworks will often sell quantities of clay for very small sums and even though it may not be suitable for pottery on its own it can give some richly textured effects when mixed with the more usual potter's clay.

Clay reclamation

All clean clay scrap, from bench scrapings to broken greenware, should be put into a bin for reclamation. After slaking, the clay slurry is spread out on a smooth and absorbent surface to stiffen. Plaster bats are ideal and can easily be cast into place on a bench or table top. The soft clay is turned regularly to hasten water loss and ensure roughly even drying before being kneaded up and returned to stock for further use.

Any contaminated clay should be thrown away or kept for use with plaster casting. Once clay has been biscuit fired it cannot be slaked and broken pieces can only be consigned to the wastebin or kept for use in glaze checks (page 75).

Kneading

Kneading is a good preliminary to wedging, especially when the clay is fragmented or varied in consistency. It is a tiring activity, so only knead small quantities which can easily be handled. A roughly compressed block is up-ended on the bench with the heel of each hand resting on top (7). Downward pressure of the hands backed by body weight forces the clay away across the bench, doubling the clay in on itself (8). Repetition of the action elongates the clay into the form of a bull's head which is then tilted on to one of its 'horns' and the process repeated.

Stiff clay can be softened by working in clay slurry. Alternate layers of clay and slurry are stacked up, the whole mass is worked together by hand and then kneaded thoroughly. Soft clay can be stiffened by working in drier clay, and the working qualities and fired appearance of the clay altered by the addition of grog, stains, and other materials.

In making any object in clay, the consistency or plasticity of the material is important. To wedge easily, to roll out sheet or coils, or to press out thumb pots needs clay which is soft enough to work easily but not so soft that it sticks to the hands, bench or tools. For slab work or constructions involving the assembly of various parts, the same clay consistency is used in the initial stages. Once the rolling and cutting is complete, the clay is left to stiffen until the pieces can be handled without distortion.

The ability to assess the correct consistency of clay for a particular project soon comes with experience, even though this may be by trial and error. The clay used for many of the pieces illustrated in this book and in the kneading/wedging sequences is a brown stoneware mix containing a small proportion of grog which appears as lighter flecks in the raw clay. The other principal clay is a fine grey stoneware used in the domestic ware and some of the very thin forms illustrated.

Once the clay has been kneaded, the separate pieces can be formed into one block and wedged up for use.

7 *The clay on end ready for the downward thrust of arms and body*

8 *The end of the thrust, with the clay showing the developing bull's head form*

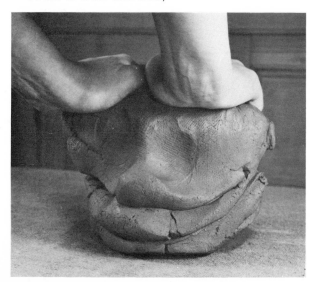

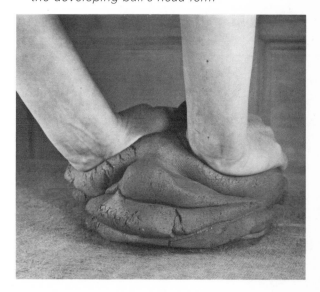

Wedging

Clay must always be thoroughly wedged, a process which expels air and produces one homogenous mass. Poor wedging can cause difficulties in working and breakage or distortion during drying and firing. Kneaded clay can be wedged up very quickly, but kneading is not an essential preliminary. The wedging surface should be of wood, concrete or similar but shiny surfaces generally attach the clay and slow the operation down.

The clay block is formed so that its width is half its length and its thickness half that of the width, these proportions being roughly constant as wedging proceeds. Begin by halving with a wedging wire (9). Pick up the half lying nearest, invert and bring it down sharply on top of the other piece (10) with the cut faces in line with each other. The hands should grip the clay partly to each side and partly on top to give greater force when striking the pieces together. Give the rejoined block a quarter turn (11) which will leave the cut faces to the right. Invert the block (12) and bring it sharply down on the bench, again using the hands to exert top pressure. The mass of clay should now be similar in shape to that at the beginning of the sequence; if it is not, repeat the final action at least once to compress the clay.

Continue wedging until the cut faces cease to show horizontal wrinkles or splits between the superimposed layers at the end of a wedging sequence. Should wedging be difficult, knead in a quantity of slurry before resuming the process. Use the wedging wire to cut away the irregular edge to leave a cleanly surfaced block of clay.

9 Halving by wedging wire

10 Striking the pieces together

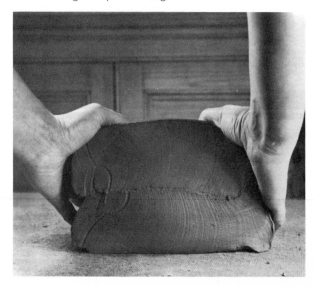

Clay benefits from aging and use; compare the working quality of a sample of new clay with some which has been wedged and rewedged over a period of time. Reclaimed clay is improved by thorough wedging and aging, even over a period of several days.

Wedging is a strenuous occupation so do not tackle a weight of clay which proves very tiring; it is far better to wedge two smaller amounts. Prepare sufficient clay for the working session.

11 *The quarter turn*

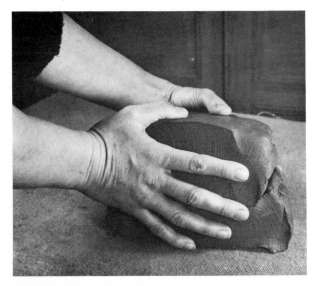

12 *Inverting the clay*

Rolling sheet clay

Many handbuilt forms require sheet clay of various uniform thicknesses. A 25 mm (1 in.) slice cut from the block of wedged clay will yield a reasonably large area when rolled out. The clay should lie on the bench as it did during wedging and the wire used horizontally to cut a layer away. If the clay is cut across the edge of the block it will split on rolling. Cutting as described means that the pressure of the roller forces the superimposed layers of clay even more firmly together.

Begin to roll from the centre of the slab (13) exerting a light and even pressure. Pick the clay up carefully and turn so that the other half can be rolled out, as well as to ensure that the clay does not adhere to the rolling surface. Continue rolling a section at a time, turning the clay sheet round on the bench. Large sheets of clay are difficult to handle without distortion and should be given as much support as possible. Rolling with the aid of two wooden lathes (14) ensures an even thickness overall and a stock of strips of various thicknesses should be kept. With experience, the lathes can often be dispensed with.

13 Beginning to roll

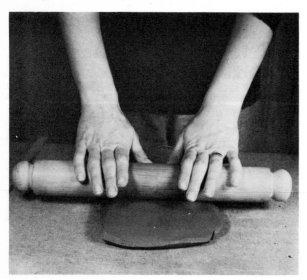

14 Using the wooden lathes

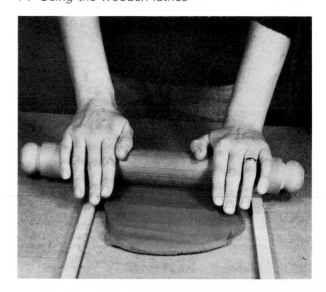

Tiles

Tiles should be cut from clay which does not warp on drying and firing; working grog into ordinary clay provides such a material. Tile cutters are available but as they are usually square in form their value is limited. Special shapes can easily be made by cutting and filing strips of metal from food cans and nailing them to wood blocks. The tile samples illustrated (15), (16), (17), (18) are just five of the possibilities open, and others include slip trailing, applied clay relief, casting, press molding and painted panels. White commercial tiles provide a good working base for ceramic enamels.

15 102 mm × 102 mm (4 in. × 4 in.) each tile Tiles impressed by a lino block and intended for assembly into sets of four. Similar designs can be completed using painted or applied decoration on sets of tiles. Glazed in white

16 Tiles impressed by the same lino block with the indentations filled with coils of soft clay in a lighter colour, scraped to the level of the tile surface. Slip can also be trailed into this type of inlaid tile. Unglazed

17 Tile 203 mm × 140 mm (8 in. × 5½ in.)
This tile was cut from a piece of thick clay
rolled on to a deeply indented plaster cast
taken from a specially prepared clay panel.
This was impressed by offcuts of wood and
the cast was made as illustrated on pages
68–9. Oxides were rubbed into the surface
of the biscuit fired tile which was then
coated with white glaze. Some of this was
rubbed off the raised areas. The deeper
depressions were filled with broken green
bottle glass which melted into pools during
firing

18 Tile 305 mm × 127 mm (12 in. × 5 in.)
Impressed decoration using two fired clay
stamps (page 76). Glazed in transparent
green

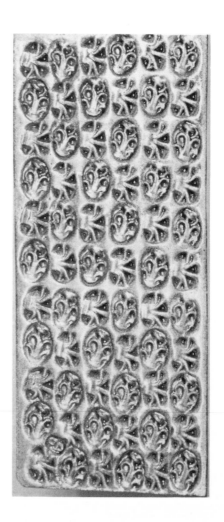

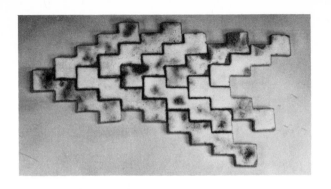

19 *Length of individual tile 95 mm (3¾ in.)*
These interlocking tiles were designed for
assembly in a variety of ways and were cut
using a knife and a card template. For large
numbers it would be possible to make a tile
cutter from strips of food-can metal
attached to a block of wood. Glazed in
white with sponge stippled copper oxide
giving a variegated surface of white, green,
and grey, with flashes of pink

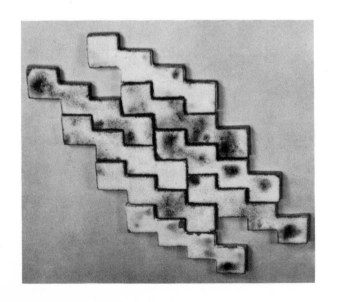

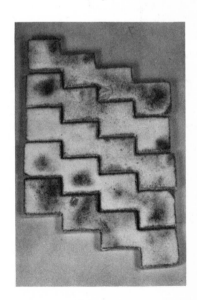

Raised edge dish

Cut a clay shape from a sheet 6 mm ($\frac{1}{4}$ in.) in thickness and place it on a small board on the bench top. Working on the farthest edge and using both hands, gently lift the edge with the fingers and apply a firm downward pressure with both thumbs (21), to crimp the clay. The rim should rise at approximately 45° to the base and be between 25 mm and 38 mm (1 in. and 1$\frac{1}{2}$ in.) in width. Move the board around slightly and form the next section, continuing the process until the whole rim is completed. Rest the knuckles of one hand on the board with the thumb inside and the fingers underneath (22), moving the hand around the rim keeping the knuckles in contact with the board. This levels the rim. Allow the dish to dry out a little before finishing with scrapers and planer files (two-way tools).

The two dishes illustrated (20) were wiped over with an iron oxide and water mixture after biscuit firing. That on the left had a design in the same oxide brushed on to the surface before being glazed in white. The other had a similar decoration brushed on the surface of the same glaze, and the fired results show the contrast between overglaze and underglaze decoration.

21 Raising the edge

22 Levelling the rim

Rectangular dish

23 Heights 54 mm to 124 mm (2⅛ in. to 4⅞ in.)

Cut a square or rectangle from a sheet of clay 6 mm ($\frac{1}{4}$ in.) thick. From the corner of a piece of thick card cut a wedge to be used as a template (24). The longer the wedge, the deeper the sides of the dish, the broader the wedge the steeper the angle of the sides.

Place the template on each corner in turn, cutting through the clay with the blade set at a slight angle (24)(25), and discarding the pieces. Cut and slip the faces of one of the joints (69) and bend up the sides (25) as for the raised edge dish on the previous page. Spread the finger tips of both hands along the length of the outside of the joint, place the thumbs inside, and press the joint firmly together (26). Repeat the process for the other joints and use a modelling tool to smooth out the joint inside and out (27) before setting the

dish aside to stiffen. If a base is to be fitted, cut the pieces out and set them aside with the dish.

Once the clay is leather hard it can be scraped down using a planer file blade (28) on the base, outside walls and rim, whilst the inside can be scraped down with a wire loop modelling tool. When working on the inside corners, support the joint carefully from the outside. Should a base be required it can now be luted into place a section at a time (29). Remember to lute the corners of the base together at the same time. Clean up the joints and set aside the completed dish to dry.

The basic design can be varied considerably according to wedge size and proportion and the form and proportion of the fitted base. There is no reason why other geometric forms such as tri-angles or hexagons cannot be treated in the same

24 Cutting the corner wedges

25 Bending up the first side

way to give multi-sided pieces. A similar technique is used to make the small bowls illustrated in figure 33.

The dishes illustrated (23) were simply glazed in either a brownish-olive glaze containing iron, or a clear bluish-green glaze containing copper.

26 *Closing the first joint*

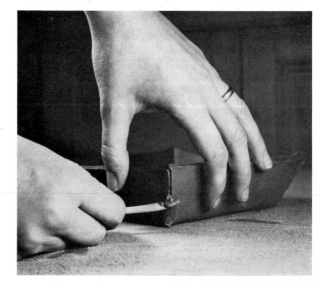

27 *Finishing outside the joint*

28 Planing the form

29 Fitting the base

Petal bowl

30 Heights 89 mm and 102 mm ($3\frac{1}{2}$ in. and 4 in.)

Cut a freehand disc from a sheet of clay less than 6 mm (¼ in.) thick and use a finger to mark a small circle around the centre to indicate the base. Place the disc on a small board which can be turned round as the work proceeds.

Use a knife to make a series of radial cuts from this finger mark to the circumference (31). The cuts may be straight or curved and the distance between them is a matter of choice but both affect the final form of the dish. Raise the farthest edge in both hands and overlap two of the petals: the greater the overlap the steeper the sides of the bowl will be (32). Lightly but firmly press the joint closed along its full length, paying particular attention to the lower end where overlap is least. Continue the process for each succeeding petal, gently curving the sides of the bowl at the same time. Close the joint seams completely with a modelling tool and use a wire loop tool to clean up the bowl when the clay is leather hard.

The bowls illustrated (30) were double glazed, the raw glaze being rubbed off corners and edges to allow the body to show through the fired glaze.

31 Cutting the petals

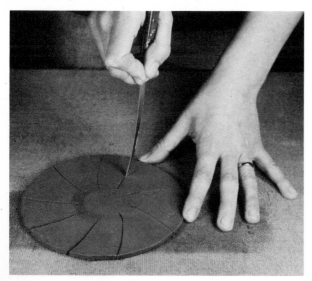

32 Joining the petals

Small bowl

Cut a disc from clay a little more than 6 mm ($\frac{1}{4}$ in.) thick and lay on a small work board. Mark an inner circle as for the petal bowl. Between this line and the edge cut and discard four curve-sided wedges (34). Work on the farthest side, lifting half the disc, curving the line of the joint and over-lapping the edges (35). Use thumb and fingers to smooth the clay together inside and out, repeating the whole sequence on the other joints.

33 Diameters 121 mm to 165 mm (4$\frac{3}{4}$ in.
       to 6$\frac{1}{2}$ in.)

Support with one hand from the outside and use the rubber kidney to help shape the bowl (36). Invert and apply hand pressure near the base to give the base of the bowl a smooth curve (37). Allow it to stiffen slightly before making final adjustments to the trueness of the rim, scraping the inside with a metal kidney, and using a planer file to finish the sides and cut a small base. The walls should taper slightly in thickness from base to rim, and all traces of the joints should have disappeared.

The two taller bowls (33) each had a strip of clay pinched on to the rim after the initial building stage. All are dip-glazed in various overlapping colours.

34 Cutting the wedges

35 Overlapping and pressing the first joint

36 Shaping with a rubber kidney

37 Completing the curve on the inverted bowl.

Hump mould

38 Diameters 184 mm (7$\frac{1}{4}$ in.)

Hump moulds can be made or adapted from a variety of materials including rounded stones, plastic bags filled with foam chippings or sawdust, plaster casts, fired clay, or carved, as in this example, where a soft aerated building block was chiselled and filed into shape. Deep moulds such as this are not so easy to work as those with gentler curves. The mould must be raised sufficiently to allow a knife to be used in cutting the clay on it.

Roll out the clay to 6 mm ($\frac{1}{4}$ in.) and from it cut a piece slightly larger than the mould in plan. Lift carefully and drape over the mould, using hand pressure (39) to form the clay closely without wrinkles or overlaps. Most of the excess clay can be cut away before the rim is pressed in on the mould.

Begin to trim the clay away with a knife (40) making sure that the rim is not curved underneath the mould and so making removal impossible. Should a base or foot be required it should be fitted at this point. The bowls illustrated each had a wide strip of clay luted into position (69) (70) and a coil of clay (83–86) faired or smoothed into the joint. The pot is left on the mould for a short time to stiffen before careful removal, finishing and drying.

The bowls (38) were simply glazed in white with a sgraffito decoration.

39 Handforming the clay on the mould

40 Cutting the rim

33

Sling mould

41 Length 413 mm (16¼ in.)

Tie a piece of open weave fabric across the four legs of an upturned chair, the corners of a box, or pieces of wood nailed upright on the corners of a rectangular board (42). Cut a curving shape from clay a little more than 6 mm ($\frac{1}{4}$ in.) thick, and centre it in the sling. Stroke firmly with a rubber kidney to shape the form (43). Once shaping is complete, allow the clay to stiffen and then remove the dish from the sling ready for final finishing. Metal kidneys can be used to scrape the inside whilst the rim and outside are finished with planer files and knives. A foot ring can be added at this point but this should have been prepared in advance and dried out at the same rate as the dish. Shape the foot to the base of the bowl and lute firmly into position, filling the angle between the two with a small coil faired into bowl and foot. Other designs of foot can, of course, be used.

The dish illustrated (41) is glazed in white. Manganese dioxide was flicked from a brush on to the raw glaze, giving a brown design on firing.

42 The sling in position

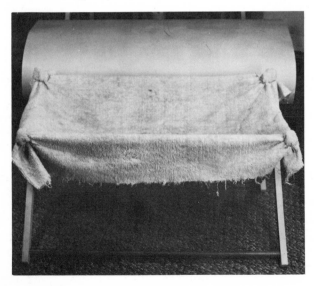

43 Shaping the clay into the sling

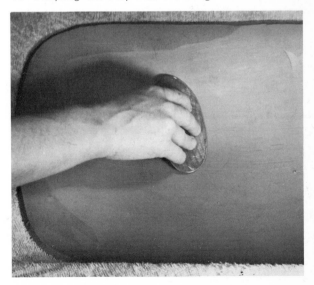

Coil mould

44 Diameters 260 mm (10¼ in.)

From a sheet of clay some 6 mm ($\frac{1}{4}$ in.) thick, cut a curving form; it need not be circular. At the same time roll a coil of clay (see figures 83–86) to a diameter of 38 mm ($1\frac{1}{2}$ in.). The edge of the clay sheet is lifted section by section and the coil pushed underneath until the whole rim is supported: cut away the excess coil. Gently ease the edge of the sheet clay into the mould with light pressure, working several times round the mould if necessary (45). Heavy pressure will simply distort the clay sheet against the coil. Use a rubber kidney to complete the curved rim, giving full support with the other hand as shaping proceeds (46) and then set aside to stiffen.

Once the dish has become leather hard the coil support can be removed and the rim planed level. A planer file or knife blade (95) is used to remove any trace of the coil from the outside, whilst a metal kidney and knife are used on the inside, before the dish is set aside to dry resting on the rim.

The illustration (44) shows the use of a paper stencil (left) and wax resist (right). A circular stencil was cut from a folded disc of paper and dampened on to the biscuit-fired dish. A purplish glaze was poured over and the stencil removed to leave clear areas of clay behind. A brown glaze was then poured over the whole interior, giving a greenish-brown with traces of blue after firing. The other had a design painted on in wax before being glazed and fired in the same purplish glaze, after which the inside was thinly coated with an iron glaze and the dish refired.

45 Easing the clay into the mould

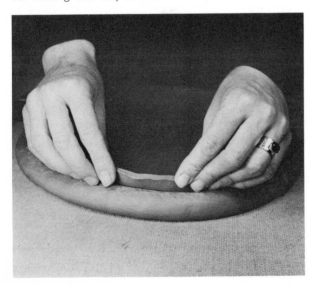

46 Shaping with the rubber kidney

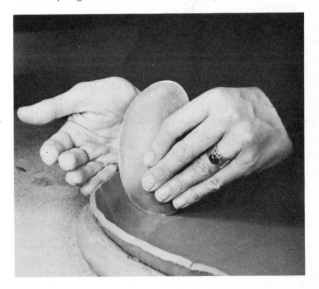

Hollow mould—slipware

47 Diameters 197 mm (7¾ in.)

Roll out clay 6 mm ($\frac{1}{4}$ in.) thick and cut a piece slightly larger than the mould. Lay this across the mould, easing it down with the fingers (48) until the clay is in contact with the base. Continue to ease the clay with one hand whilst gently sponging the clay close to the sides of the mould with the other (49). Do not stretch the clay into place with the sponge as this can cause splits during firing. The sponge should be damp but not wet. Trim most of the excess clay off and give the rim of the dish a final circuit with the sponge.

To trim the remaining clay, hold a knife in one hand with the blade pressed flat on top of the mould, whilst the other hand holds the sponge against the clay to keep it in place as cutting begins. Using the knuckle of the index finger as a pivot, turn the knife blade to cut the clay against the mould (50) to remove some 25 mm (2 in.) of clay at a time. Continue until the whole rim is cut level then sponge lightly to remove roughness and the sharp edge.

Use a white slip of creamy consistency as the base, pouring a quantity into the mould. Pick this up and roll the slip up to the rim, turning the mould until the clay is covered (51). Tip the excess out, placing the thumbs across the mould to retain the dish (52). The mould should be held at a 45° angle as the slip is emptied with sharp, straight jerks (52). Use a clean sponge to clean the slip off the rim without allowing any to run down into the dish.

Fill the slip trailers by holding their mouths under the surface of the slip, squeezing to expel the air which is then replaced by slip. Wipe clean and insert a nozzle in each, testing to see that the slip flows freely. Hold the slip trailer in both hands with elbows resting on the bench and trail even strips of slip across the dish at intervals (53).

Apply the second colour between the lines of the first (54) before knocking the mould gently on the bench to flatten the trails. Draw the thin springy tip of a stripped feather across the trails at regular intervals, turning the mould to repeat the lines in the opposite direction (55). In the examples illustrated (47) the base of the feather was used for the press pattern on the rim. The right hand dish was trailed as the mould was rotated on a banding wheel (see glossary). Once feathering is complete, the mould is set aside until the dish is stiff enough to be removed without distortion. After biscuit firing, a clear honey coloured glaze was applied to finish the ware.

Slip trailing has a long history and examples can be studied in books and museums. A slip trailer may be used as a drawing instrument, albeit a rather coarse one. By using a combination of lines, dots, and several colours, the ware can be decorated with abstract or naturalistic designs, or a combination of the two. Once the consistency of the slip and the handling of the slip trailer become familiar, the decorative possibilities are very wide. The slip can also be trailed directly onto the clay without a preliminary base coat. The technique can be adapted to hump moulds. Then the decoration is applied to flat sheets of clay which are allowed to stiffen before being formed on to shallow hump moulds.

48 Easing the clay into the mould

49 Sponging and easing the clay

50 Trimming the rim

51 Applying the base slip

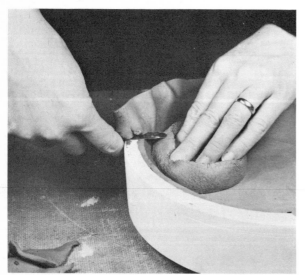

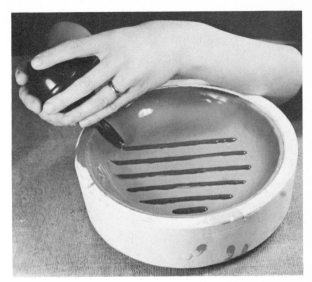

52 *Pouring off the excess slip*

53 *Trailing the first coloured slip*

54 *Trailing the second slip*

55 *Using the stripped feather*

41

56 Heights 210 mm to 251 mm (8¼ in. to 9⅞ in.)

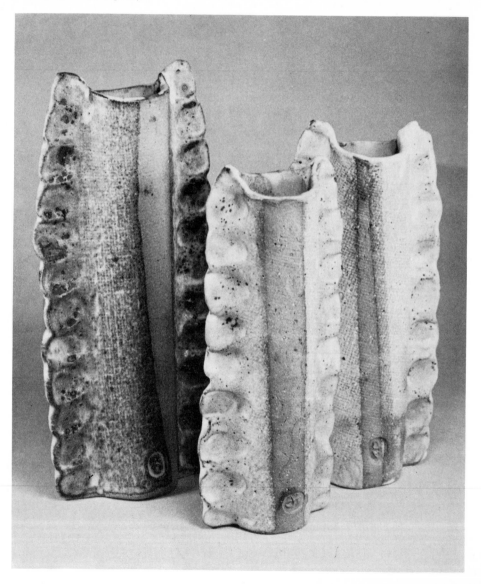

Core mould—flange joints

Cut two rectangles of clay 6 mm ($\frac{1}{4}$ in.) thick, the length of which is the height of the finished pot and the width some $2\frac{1}{2}$ to 3 times the diameter of the core, which is in this instance a cardboard tube. Lay this along the centre line of one of the slabs and superimpose the second. Working along each flange at the same time, insert the fingers between the bench and the edges of the lower sheet and lightly join to the upper with pressure between thumb and fingers. Begin at the centre of the flanges, working outwards to each end in turn. Then, one flange at a time, press the two layers firmly together (57) to make a permanent joint with the pressure points spaced out evenly along its length. Complete the second flange and trim one end of the pot as the base. Into this lute a closely fitting disc of clay, smoothing the end with a finger tip (58). Remove from the core and set aside to stiffen before completing any necessary trimming. The technique can be adapted to cores of various cross sections and the forms can incorporate a single flange or more than two of them.

The flanges of the biscuited cylinders (56) were rubbed with chrome oxide before being dipped into a thin white glaze. This has produced a glazed finish almost transparent in parts, with the chrome giving a fawn cast, speckled in a strong green.

57 Joining a flange

58 Fitting the base

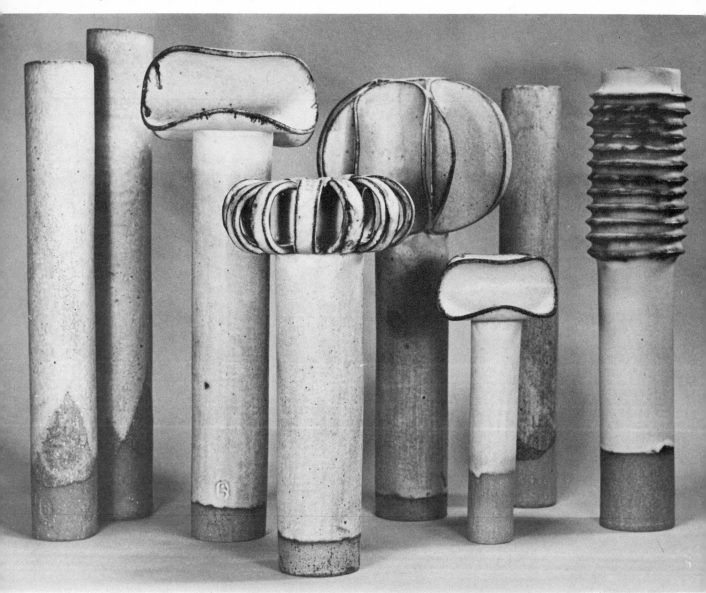

Core mould—seam joints

This technique can be used with a variety of core materials and cross sections, although those with sharp edges or angles must be used with care. To prevent the clay from sticking to the core during construction, wrap a single layer of thin polythene (polyethylene) around the core before fitting the clay into place.

For most core moulds the usual 6 mm ($\frac{1}{4}$ in.) thick clay can be used, with thicker gauges for particularly large or incised forms. From the sheet clay cut two parallel edges which will form the top and bottom of the pot, and square off a third side. Place the core along this edge and begin to roll the clay on to it (60). Tuck the edge well in and at each end mark the contact point between the edge and the clay lying on the bench (61): cut between the marks with knife and straight edge.

Replace on the mould to check for size (62), cutting away excess or lightly rolling out as necessary. Remove the clay carefully and wrap the polythene into place with the ends tucked in tidily (not shown here). Roll the clay on to the core again, cupping it in the hands and drawing the edges of the joint tightly together with the thumbs (63). Begin in the centre and work out to each end in turn. Smooth the joint out with light finger pressure (64). Stand the cylinder on a piece of scrap sheet, cut out the base with a knife (65) and lute into position (66). Scrape the joint down with knife or scraper (67). Stand the cylinder on its base, withdraw the core and peel away the polythene sheet.

Complete any press decoration or lute other pieces of clay (handles for example) into place before removing the core. Cutting through (142) or the addition of sections to the top should be done when the clay is leather hard. Curving forms can be made from sections cut away from cylinders and luted together (123).

This technique can also be adapted to produce domestic ware including candle holders (122), mugs and jugs (132), teapots (136)(141), and storage jars (140).

The cylinders illustrated (59) are simply glazed in white with the sparing addition of metallic oxides on some of them. The cylinder on the extreme right was completed by coiling directly on to the core to form the pinched fins. Apart from the plain versions, three of the examples had curved discs of clay luted into place and a fourth was cut and formed.

60 Rolling the clay on to the core

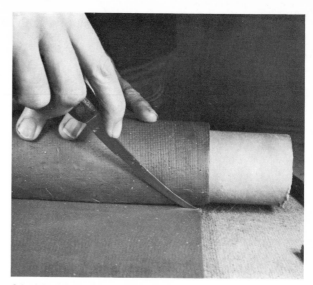

61 Marking the contact points

62 Checking the joint closure

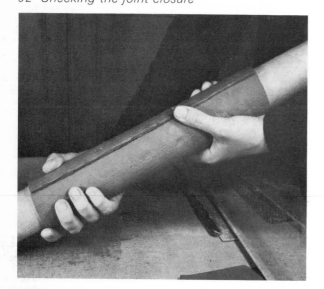

63 Closing the joint with the thumbs

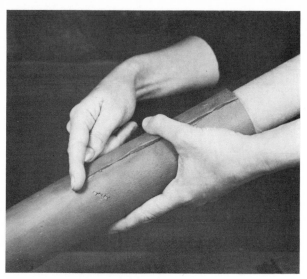

64 *Smoothing the joint*

65 *Cutting the base*

66 *Fitting the base*

67 *Finishing the joint*

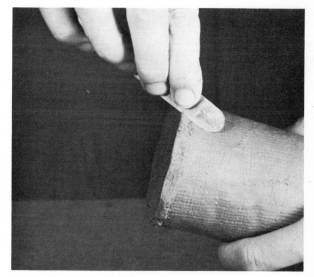

Slab building

For a simple slab pot around 305 mm (12 in.) high, cut four sides and a base from clay 6 mm ($\frac{1}{4}$ in.) thick and set aside to stiffen, until they can easily be handled without distortion. Before beginning assembly check the trueness of sides and angles, trimming as necessary.

Begin with one of the broad sides to which the two narrow sides will be joined. Apply a thick slip of clay and equal parts water and vinegar to both faces of the first joint and then complete a series of closely spaced knife cuts along the length of each (69). Brush in a little more slip before bringing the sides together with their edges in alignment. Firm pressure from the palms of both hands which hold the slab lightly between fingers and thumbs begins to close the joint (70) followed by a more even pressure from the timber lathe (71). Excessive pressure will either distort the side or force the joint apart rather than together. Clean the inside of the joint with a wooden modelling tool (72). Add the second narrow side in the same way, checking that both are at right angles to the side acting as a construction base. Check the fit of the fourth side, slip and cut the faces of both joints and press into position (73). Use the strip of wood to clean the inside of the joints, and a wooden modelling tool to finish off all four joint exteriors (74). If necessary, trim the end to be used as a base before standing it upright on the piece. Trim this to size and lute into position on the upturned form (75). Clean this joint, trim the rim, and set the pot aside to stiffen further. The whole form can then be filed and scraped (76) to give the final finish. Dry out slowly to avoid the joints splitting but should this happen they can be repaired with a thick slip of vinegar and clay.

The illustration (68) shows a selection of fairly simple slabbed forms which utilize pressed decoration, applied decoration, piercing, and assembly of various pre-formed units. Slab pots need not be rectangular and may have any number of sides (146) or be built from pieces of curved clay (2). Large or difficult forms may be built and fired in sections before being assembled with the aid of glue (2). Slab construction may also be used in conjunction with other techniques. Whatever the form or complexity involved, success lies in careful preparation and stiffening of the various parts and firm bonding together. Complete as much finishing work as possible as construction proceeds as it is usually more difficult after the form is completed.

Architecture is an obvious source of inspiration, but freer shapes can be found in plants, shells and seeds.

69 Cutting and slipping the first joint

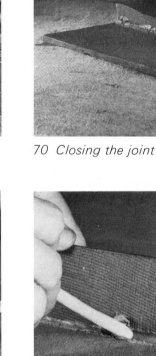

70 Closing the joint

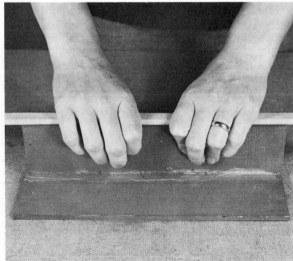

71 Using the wooden lathe

72 Cleaning the inside of the joint

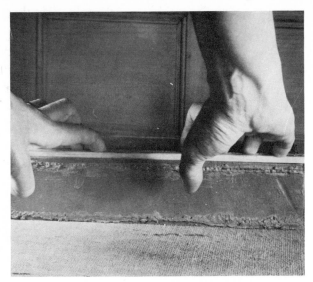

73 *Fitting the fourth side into position*

74 *Cleaning the outside of a joint*

75 *Fitting the base into position*

76 *Preliminary scraping*

Thumb pots

77 Diameters 51 mm to 108 mm (2 in. to 4¼ in.)

Thumb pots are usually small in scale, but with experience can be worked up into bowls of considerable diameter. They can also be used as the basis of a coil pot or further construction, and can be joined in pairs to produce a hollow form (128).

Take a small block of soft, thoroughly wedged clay and form into a ball between the palms of the hands. Press one thumb through the centre of the ball and begin to squeeze the clay gently between thumb and fingers (78), rotating the pot slowly to keep the walls an even thickness and the form balanced. Once the initial opening out is completed, the thumb action changes to a spiralling stroke (79) which thins the clay, forms the inside curvature, and smooths the inside surface at the same time. Concentrate on giving the inside the finished form and leave the base slightly thicker than the walls. Splits may develop in the rim but these can easily be smoothed away by drawing the edges together with finger strokes. Work quickly as the heat of the hands begins to dry the clay out and makes cracks more likely. Once forming is complete, set the pot aside to stiffen before scraping down the outside, levelling the rim, and filing a small base.

The thumb pots illustrated (77) have been used in glaze testing and decorative experiments, all confined to their interiors.

78 Opening out the clay

79 Smoothing and shaping the inside

Scoop pots

Cut a block of soft clay and press into a curving, but not necessarily spherical, form between the hands. Halve with a wedging wire and use a wire loop modelling tool to scoop out the insides (80) which are then smoothed with the thumb. Pierce a small hole in one of the portions to allow air to escape when they are rejoined. Cut and slip the faces of the joint and press the two pieces together between the hands (81), smoothing out the joint. After the form has been allowed to stiffen a design can be cut into the thick 13 mm ($\frac{1}{2}$ in.) clay.

The forms illustrated are based on plant seeds, and had various oxides rubbed into their surfaces before biscuit firing. Glaze was then wiped over them with a sponge which produced a slight sheen after the glost firing.

Similar forms can be made from two thumb pots joined together (128), that being the better method when deeply incised designs are not planned. The jointing method is exactly the same but greater care is needed as the forms are much thinner. They should be an exact fit, rim to rim, and should be luted together when leather-hard. Small bowls with deeply incised walls can be made using this scoop technique.

80 Scooping out the clay

81 Joining the halves together

82 *Diameters approximately 64 mm to 89 mm
(2½ in. to 3½ in.)*

Coil pots

Rolling the coils

Cut thoroughly wedged clay into 25 mm (1 in.) slices, reduce each to strips of the same width and some 102 mm (4 in.) in length and stack them ready for rolling. Begin by giving the block a roughly circular cross section by squeezing in the hand (83). Lay the stubby coil on the bench and begin to roll it backwards and forwards using the full length of palm and fingers (84). Work slowly and steadily, and if the coil begins to flatten press it back into shape. As rolling proceeds, work from the centre of the coil moving the hands away from each other to draw the coil out to its full length. Concentrate on maintaining a constant diameter along the coil and avoid pressure on any narrow section (85). Should the coil become very long it can be cut to make completion easier.

For most pots, the coil thickness illustrated is adequate but should be adjusted for small and very large pots. Thick coils contribute little extra to the strength of a pot and a considerable amount of weight, so it is best to use fairly thin coils to give a pot which is light and pleasant to handle. It may be necessary to stop more frequently to let the clay stiffen than when using thick coils but this is a small disadvantage. Once rolling is complete, the only action remaining is to cut the open clay from each end of the coil (86). Roll a good supply of coils before beginning to build and keep them covered with polythene or a damp cloth until needed. Coil rolling may be difficult to begin with, but a period of practice should enable

83 Squeezing the clay block

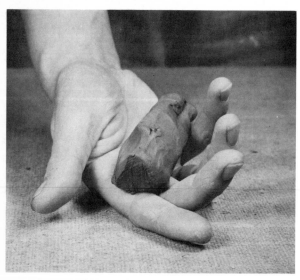

84 Beginning to roll the coil

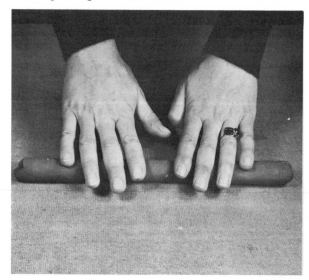

smooth and regular lengths to be produced.

Coils can be useful in building other pots when used as a fillet or strengthener. For example, the foot ring on the hump mould bowl (38) had a coil faired into the joint between it and the bowl itself to produce a smoothly flowing form.

Coil building

Once a good supply of coils has been prepared, cut a base from sheet clay and begin by placing the first coil. Hold the coil by one end and guide the other into place with the fingers of the second hand (88). Press the coil firmly into place with the thumb to join it to the clay below and to provide a flat base for the succeeding layer. Gradually ease the coils away from the centre to increase the diameter with each successive circuit and stopping every six to eight layers to join them together (89). Cup one hand under the rim to support the walls and use the index finger of the other to push down through each coil to merge them together. The pot can then be inverted and the same treatment given to the outside.

Continue to coil (90) giving plenty of support from the hand used to lay the coils in place, and stopping at six or eight layer intervals to join them together. Use a rubber kidney to smooth the inside as building progresses (91). As the coils are fitted into place the whole form can be rotated so that the hand used to place the coils is always in a comfortable working position: stand the pot on a small board or a banding wheel to make it easier.

85 The final stages of rolling

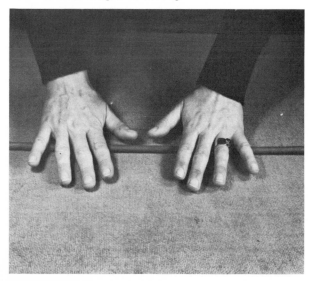

86 Trimming the end of the coil

Once the widest point has been reached the coils are eased in towards the centre with each successive layer (92) and at this stage they can be reduced in diameter slightly. A palette knife or modelling tool can substitute for a finger on the outside (93) but unless the pot is very large all merging on the inside must be done by finger. This can be awkward in a narrow necked pot such as this, but it must be done as thoroughly as possible. As the final part of the pot is reached the coils can be much thinner than lower down the form (94) or can be replaced by strips of clay pinched and formed with the fingers. When coiling is completed the outside can be given a light preliminary scrape (95) before the pot is loosely covered in polythene and left to stiffen. Remember that a coil pot cannot always be completed in one session, especially when built up from thin coils. As soon as the form shows signs of distortion allow it to stiffen a little but keep the rim covered with a strip of damp cloth to keep it soft for the next coil. Should the rim harden, lute the next coil firmly into place and resume coiling as before. Once the clay is leather hard the pot can be scraped to its final finish and dried out slowly and evenly. If thin coils are used in building, very little clay should be removed at this stage.

Coiling is a versatile method of construction and with experience it is possible to build large or complex forms very quickly indeed. The coils themselves can be left unsmoothed, with a modelling tool or finger pinching (130) used to join them together to produce a deeply textured surface. Pots may be beaten with a strip of wood to change their form (129) or be a combination of coiling and other techniques (139).

Strip building

Flat strips cut from sheets of rolled clay can be used to build large thin-walled forms very rapidly and with little need for final fettling. This technique is best reserved for amply curved pieces over 305 mm (12 in.) in height where it is significantly faster than conventional coiling. The two methods can be combined. The strips may be as wide as 51 mm (2 in.) or more depending on the overall dimensions of the piece. They are built up directly from a base to which three or four layers of coils have been added, each strip being placed inside that immediately below it to give an overlap. Fingers and thumb are used to pinch the strips together as soon as they are in place, as well as to shape the form at the same time. Inside and outside are fettled as the building proceeds.

The pots illustrated (87) were based on gourd forms and had metallic oxides rubbed dry into the bisque ware before the application of a white glaze.

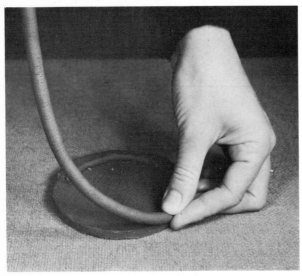

88 *Placing the first coil on the base*

90 *Continuing to coil*

89 *Joining the coils together*
91 *Using the rubber kidney to shape the form,
giving support to the outside*

92 Turning the coils to begin the taper towards the neck

93 Using a palette knife to join the coils together

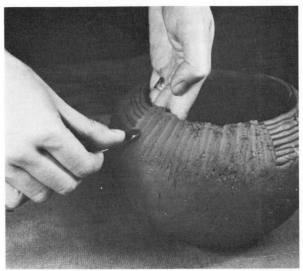

94 Placing thinner coils to form the neck

95 Scraping the outside of the finished form

Design

The design of pottery forms and their decoration should be backed by collections of inspirational material compiled as scrapbooks, photographs, slides, notebooks, sketch pads and found objects, as well as direct observation of the day-to-day environment. A basic scrapbook can be made from sheets of stout paper folded centrally and tied with string into a card cover. It can contain magazine illustrations, photographs, postcards and other material showing forms, patterns and textures of interest to the collector and not necessarily connected closely to pottery. A separate book can be kept for illustrations of pottery from the past and illustrated pamphlets from pottery manufacturers. Slides can be used in a small battery-operated viewer. Written notes recording completed practical work and experiments, or summaries from pottery handbooks, are easy to maintain. Sketch pads have a dual role, being used for studies of pottery displayed in museums and objects observed in the environment as well as in the design process itself. Ideas and themes can be developed quickly in sketch form before translation into clay, and full pads should always be kept as they often provide useful ideas long after the sketches are completed. Shelf space in the pottery should be set aside for displays of found objects as well as an area of wall board on which to pin material not committed to a scrapbook.

When a promising theme has been discovered, it should be fully explored in sketch and in clay, working freely to evolve a series of ideas until the potential appears exhausted. Consider the pieces as a family of closely related members, similar in appearance yet not identical in form; examples of 'families' are illustrated throughout this book. Working in this way is often more rewarding than any other and it also allows for the inevitable disappointments which emerge from the glost firing. The design and decoration of each piece must be considered as a whole and sketches or written notes compiled as a reference when preparations are made for the glost firing. Familiarity with clay building techniques and a wide range of decorative processes is also an essential part of the design process.

Design sources for pieces illustrated include: architecture (4) (142) (143) (145) (146); fruits and seeds (1) (80) (87) (119); bollards (139); tree bark (131); museum exhibits (5); plant stems (125) (127) (131); and marine forms (137).

Techniques

Many of the handbuilt techniques described require sheet clay as the basis for construction and often a thickness of 6 mm ($\frac{1}{4}$ in.) is prescribed. This is intended as a general guide and can be increased or decreased according to the overall dimensions of the pot. Try to assess the thickness of clay appropriate to each piece, both technically and visually. Some forms look very light whilst others appear solid and heavy but in both cases their individual construction should reflect this visual feeling. Contradictions do happen and can be disconcerting when the pot is handled. Using thick clay is not necessarily going to produce a stronger pot, especially in the early building stages when the clay is plastic. The quality of the clay in use is important and its plasticity must be appropriate to the use envisaged. Clay ideal for immediate use in a coil pot is useful for slabwork only after the pieces have been cut and left to stiffen for some time. Some of the forms illustrated are difficult to make if the clay is too soft or too hard, either collapsing or splitting during construction.

When joining pieces together, luting may or may not be necessary. It is essential on a slab pot but only occasionally on a coil pot, for example. In both cases the separate parts must be bonded together so as to become one. When luting pieces together, begin by brushing the area of the joint with a thick slip, make a series of closely spaced knife cuts around 3 mm ($\frac{1}{8}$ in.) in depth, brush in a further quantity of slip and end by pressing the joint firmly closed and scraping the excess slip away. Remember that clay shrinks as it dries and that soft clay luted to hard is almost certain to break away because of this. Always ensure that all parts are of the same plasticity and therefore have the same latent shrinkage. Likewise, dry large or complex pieces slowly and evenly to avoid cracks or distortion.

Selection of the appropriate technique is important and there is little point in using a particular technique for the sake of using it when another would simplify construction. It may be that a form is best made from a combination of techniques (5) or assembled from various sections all of which use the same technique. The choice of clay is important visually; a small mug in a coarse, gritty clay would be clumsy in appearance and rough to use, while a rugged sculptural form in a fine clay might seem lifeless. The following six pages deal with the detail techniques of lids, handles and spouts, as well as the making of hollow moulds in plaster of Paris.

Handles

Handles can be difficult to design for a particular pot, each requiring the consideration of form and proportion. They can be pulled from coils of clay, cut from flat sheet, hollow in cross section, or made from a material other than clay. A handle must be visually pleasing as well as comfortable to hold in any position required by use and, in certain instances, designed to protect the user. Any containers used for cooking or holding hot liquids must have handles which are easy to grip with protective gloves or handles which keep the user's fingers away from the hot areas.

Pulled handles are easy to make from thick coils of clay and, provided shape and proportion are good, give a simple yet pleasing form. The coil is either held in the hands or, as in the example illustrated (96), laid flat on the bench. Stroking pressure from wet fingers soon gives the coil the designed taper and the embryo handle is trimmed roughly to size and bent on to the bench to stiffen. The body and handle can be made at the same time and should be dried out at the same rate. After final trimming and shape adjustment, the handle is luted into place (97). Until experience is gained it is as well to make more than one handle for each pot to allow for failures in either form or attachment. The handle should need little finishing once it is in place, providing the pulling is carefully done. Coil handles can also be straight and attached at one end only.

Slab handles are quick and easy to make (98) (99), but should be used with care. Strap handles can be fitted to domestic ware and are rather

96 Pulling a handle

97 Fitting a handle

similar to pulled handles in outline and fitting. As the name suggests, they are wide and flat with a slight increase in thickness down the centre of the strip. Hollow handles can be used on ovenware to help dissipate heat. Core mould techniques can be adapted to give the necessary shape to the handle. Other materials such as bamboo, wood, cane (100), can be used for handle making.

Thick basketmakers' cane was used for this handle fitted to clay lugs on the body. The cane was first trimmed to size, and the ends were thinned down with a sharp knife, before being soaked in boiling water until pliable. The handle was then shaped after which the ends were fitted through the lugs and bound into place with thin brown twine. Ready-made handles of this and other material can be obtained commercially.

98 Slab handle on teapot (136) *99 Slab handle on casserole (133)* *100 Cane handle on teapot (142)*

 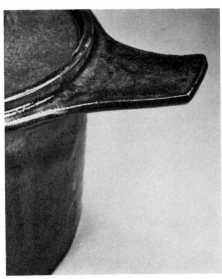 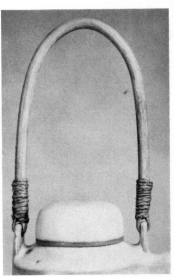

Lids

Two basic types of lid are illustrated in close-up. The first (101) is made from two discs of clay luted together, the larger resting on the rim of the storage jar and the smaller a close fit within the rim. A knob or handle could be added, especially if the lid is wide enough to make it difficult to pick up. The second (102) fits into the storage jar to rest on a ledge formed from a strip of clay luted into position. The lid itself is a single disc of clay to which a knob carved from a coil of clay has been added. Both examples come from the storage jars illustrated in (140). Other lids illustrated include a cork in another storage jar, a disc with ring handle on a casserole (133), a disc with locating tab on a teapot (136), and a domed teapot lid made up from a thumb pot (141).

The third lid shown here (103) is also on a storage jar and the same technique is applied to the candle holder (122). The clay cylinder was closed at both ends after which the joint between lid and body was marked out with a pair of dividers and cut with a sharp knife.

101 Double disc lid (140)

102 Single disc lid with carved knob (140)

103 Lid interlocking with container (140)

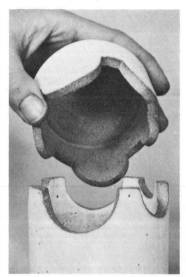

Lips and spouts

Lips are formed as soon as construction is complete and while the clay remains relatively soft. The fingers of one hand support the rim whilst the thumb of the other is used to draw the lip gently out (104). A broad gently curving lip like this one pours better than one with a narrower form; this example is from the jug in illustration (132).

The centre illustration (105) shows a spout built up from two triangular slabs of thin clay and is from the teapot illustrated on page 89. The holes in the body of the pot were cut with a small woodworking drill. Before the teapot was raw glazed the holes were covered with wax to keep them clear of glaze.

The second spout (106) is also from a teapot (141). A small sheet of thin clay was formed into a cylinder on a wood dowel core, allowed to stiffen, and finally trimmed and luted into position. The full form was completed by adding small quantities of clay towards the base of the spout which was then finished off with a knife blade. The lip was gently pinched to give it a slight flair.

104 *Forming the lip on a jug (132)*

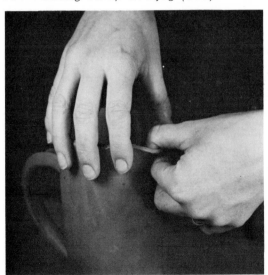

105 *Slabbed teapot spout (136)*

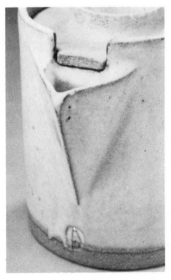

106 *Core mould teapot spout (141)*

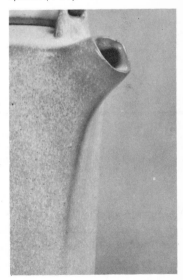

Plaster moulds

Design the mould on paper, drawing a plan and a cross-section through the centre. Transfer the plan to a piece of hardboard or plywood, marking it clearly with a thick black line. Use tinsnips to cut a metal sheet into a profile based on the cross-section (107). Pack soft clay firmly on to the board until there is sufficient to begin trimming it down to the designed form.

Use the profile scraper (107), working round the form until the drawn line on the hardboard is exposed and the contours are smooth and even. Build a retaining wall from metal, linoleum, plastic or card (108), leaving a gap of 25 mm (1 in.) between it and the clay form. Roll out a thick coil and press firmly into the angle between wall and base board to seal the gap.

Estimate the amount of plaster needed to cover the clay form to a depth of 19–25 mm ($\frac{3}{4}$–1 in.) and pour the appropriate quantity of water into a bowl. Sprinkle fine plaster of Paris into the centre of the bowl where it should quickly settle in the water. Continue until the plaster breaks the surface and then begin to sprinkle in the outer areas of the bowl (109). Stir lightly with a stick as the last handfuls of powder are added, but be careful to avoid the formation of lumps in the mixture. When it begins to thicken, it should be poured quickly into the enclosure and the base-board should be bumped several times on the bench to settle the plaster. Use a straight edge to level the plaster (110) which will begin to set almost immediately. Once setting is complete, remove the retaining wall, lift the cast from the

107 Using the metal profile

108 Building the retaining wall

board and scoop out the clay form. Scrapers can then be used to finish off the plaster surface and chamfer the sharp edges before the mould is left to dry out.

Clay contaminated with plaster must NOT be used for pot making or returned to the clay stock. Waste plaster should not be flushed away in the sink but scraped on to old newspaper and consigned to the wastebin (garbage pail).

Commercial suppliers usually stock ready-made moulds but these are often small and sometimes difficult to use. Moulds are easy to make in a wide variety of forms, although deep sections should be avoided as they are difficult to work with sheet clay.

109 Preparing the plaster

110 Levelling the base of the mould

Finishing and biscuit firing

Fettling

Through care in cutting, forming and jointing the clay pieces, much of the finishing work can be completed as the forms are made. Some operations are easier to execute when the clay has reached a point in drying out where although it is no longer flexible, it can still be worked with metal tools without breaking up. These tools may be used on the leather-hard clay to finish forms and surfaces (95), to cut surface reliefs (80), or to pierce the clay completely (142). Care must be taken to avoid unwanted holes or excessively thin walls in the piece being fettled. Use sharp tools, cut a little away at a time, always give plenty of support to the working area, and when working on an edge or rim, cut along the length of it rather than across it. Broken pieces can usually be successfully rejoined by luting them together with vinegared slip.

Drying out

Small or simple pieces can safely be left out to dry on open shelving unless the room temperature is high. Avoid placing pieces where they would be subjected to strong sunlight or heat from radiators, both of which will cause uneven drying and the consequent risk of cracks and warps. Larger pieces, especially those assembled from several parts, are best covered loosely with polythene bags or sheeting and allowed to dry out slowly and evenly. Flatware (pots where the diameter of the rim is greater than anywhere else on the form) should be dried on the rim to eliminate risk of distortion. Rapid or uneven drying sets up stresses which may warp or break the piece during drying, or later, in the kiln. It is very difficult to mend breakages in dry ware but if the pieces are carefully luted together with vinegared slip and the joint burnished with a wooden tool as it dries, repairs can be successful. When the pot is completely dry the surface may, if necessary, be finely finished using glasspaper or wire wool. Shrinkage takes place as the clay dries out.

Biscuit firing

As soon as the greenware is completely dry, it is ready for biscuit firing. Suppliers' catalogues give firing temperatures for their clays and these should be followed. Earthenware and stoneware can be packed together in the same firing. Pack the pieces closely without putting them into contact with kiln walls or roof, placing small items inside large and stacking wherever possible. Close packing saves kiln space but remember the fragility of greenware and handle it accordingly. Keep large, flat-sided, or very thin pots away from the elements to avoid distortion during firing. Flat slabs can be bedded in silver sand, spread on the kiln shelf. Begin with a survey of the pieces to be packed and attempt to work out a plan which places them throughout the kiln. Place the props for the second layer of shelves at the same time as packing is begun on the bottom shelves, adjusting for height and adding the next shelf when the lower space is filled. Continue to build up the props, shelves and ware until the packing is complete. Plastic clay is used to fill any gap which may occur between a shelf and the top of a column of props. If cones are to be used for temperature checks they should be set in plastic clay and placed in the kiln where they are visible through the spy-hole in the door. Place two cones, one which will collapse at the required temperature and the second a little below, giving advance warning that firing is almost complete. Close and padlock the door, switch on to low power or set the cut-out to a low reading and leave overnight, making sure that the bungs in the roof and door are not in place.

Lingering traces of water in the clay are soon driven off, and organic materials begin to burn out at around 250°C as the power is slowly increased the following day. Water is also chemically combined with the clay particles and is released as the kiln temperature moves from approximately 350° to 550°C. Temperature increase should be slow at this stage while the water is driven off as steam and must work its way out of the clay body; too rapid a rise can result in shattered pots. Once 600°C is passed, the kiln can be worked up to full power with the bungs inserted. The biscuit temperature will be reached fairly quickly, at which point the power is switched off and the kiln left to cool. Open and unpack the now biscuit-fired ware only when it can be handled comfortably. Biscuit-fired pots, like greenware, are fragile, and should be moved and stored carefully in cupboards or covered up to exclude dust. At this stage the body is porous.

111 *Kiln packed for a glost firing with the last shelf yet to be placed. The cones can be seen in the centre of the upper shelf. All the tall pieces are packed at the back whilst the front shelves carry a variety of forms and sizes*

112 *Kiln and glazing equipment*

Kiln and glazing equipment

1 Stilts   Stilts are used in glost firings to separate the pots from kiln shelves where there is risk of the glaze flowing off the base of the pot. They should be placed with care so that the piece is evenly balanced and in stoneware firings should be used sparingly because of possible distortion of thin pieces.

2 Props   The castellated props illustrated are one of several types used in shelf stacking. Three or four columns are used for each shelf or more when it is thought that a shelf might sag under a particularly heavy pot. When a shelf is warped and sits unevenly on the columns of props a plug of clay can be inserted between the shelf and the top of one of the stacks. Make certain that the shelves are stable as packing proceeds.

3 Brushes   A wide variety of brush forms is available for use in decorating ware.

4 Lawn and brush   Lawns (sieves) are used in the preparation of slips and glazes and can be bought graded according to the mesh size. An 80 or 100 mesh lawn is sufficient for general use in the pottery. The lawn brush shown has coconut bristles strapped to a wooden handle but a nylon domestic brush can be substituted if necessary.

Kiln shelves   The purchase and treatment of kiln shelves is covered in the section on equipment.

Temperature cones   The use of temperature cones is described in the section on glaze application and firing, and illustrated in (116).

Glaze and slip preparation

Mixing

Glazes bought direct from the suppliers only require mixing with water and sieving to prepare them for use. Those mixed up to a special recipe must have the individual ingredients measured carefully into the glaze container before mixing can begin. After adding the water, give the mixture a preliminary stir with a piece of wood before using a hand to break up the lumps which invariably form, and brush through an 80 or 100 mesh lawn (112). Dilute further if the glaze is too thick. Should it be too thin, allow the glaze to settle for 24 hours and decant the surface water. Always sieve a glaze which has not been used for some time and remember to check the consistency before beginning a glazing session. This can be done by dipping a piece of broken biscuit ware into the glaze and assessing the thickness of the raw glaze picked up.

Slips are prepared in the same way, with colouring stains included in the dry ingredients before the addition of water.

Glaze and slip colourants

Manufacturers supply glaze and slip stains under their own brand names. These stains contain metal oxides and earth materials and give a specified colour when added to a base glaze as a stated percentage.

All the coloured glazes used in the book were prepared by adding small percentages of metal oxides to a basic white glaze which is also extensively used. It is difficult to predict the precise colour to be expected from a particular oxide in a glaze as this is affected by the composition of the glaze itself and the firing temperature. The following table gives an indication of the colours produced by four basic oxides when added singly to a glaze batch; as a general rule a colour becomes stronger or deeper as the percentage of oxide is increased. (Space precludes a table setting out the results of oxides in combination.)

Black copper oxide	up to 5%	greys/greens/ blacks
Red iron oxide (hematite)	up to 10%	tans/browns/ blacks
Cobalt oxide	up to 2%	blue
Manganese oxide	up to 7%	light brown/ brown/ purplish brown

Glaze testing

When glaze samples or a batch of raw glaze has been freshly mixed, test firings should be made. Pieces of broken tile or pot, thumb pots or specially made tiles (113) can be used to check the glaze performance under a variety of conditions. Such a standardized test piece is by far the best way to carry firing samples. The tile has a thumb pot attached, an area of press decoration, the glaze number brushed on in metal oxide, and is drilled in the top corners for wall display. It has been dipped into raw glaze to the incised line, and dipped for a second time to the half-way mark to test the reaction of one glaze fired over another. These test tiles can be used to check single glazes, underglaze slips, overglaze decoration, and other decorative techniques described on pages 76–78. A display of standardized tests gives clear information on the performance of a new batch of an established glaze as well as providing a record of successful glaze experiments. Careful records should be maintained showing the full recipe or supplier's catalogue number, firing temperature and other relevant information. A hardcover book is adequate but a card index is better when glaze experiments are frequent.

113 *Test tile showing the result of combining two glazes. The upper glazed section carries a coating of brown glaze whilst the lower carries the same glaze coated with one which, when fired alone, is bluish purple. The combination is a mixture of very dark blue and brownish black*

Decoration

The three sections, clay, slip, and glaze, summarize many of the decorative processes open to the potter. Examples of some of these techniques are indicated by their illustration number, and each finished pot illustrated has information on its decoration included in the caption.

Clay

Fingers Deep textures are produced by pinching the clay between finger and thumb (130), or by pressing fingers or knickles into it.

Objects Tools, rough stones, pieces of wood, ruler edges, machine parts, and other objects can be pressed into the surface (113).

Stamps Pieces of clay pressed on to objects record their surface texture which can then be reproduced on any pot once the stamp has been biscuited (18) (68). Small plaster casts can be taken from the impressions left by objects applied to soft clay, to be used in the same way.

Rollers Discs of wood, plastic, or plaster, each with a carved edge and fitted into a simple wire handle, give a linear design when rolled across the clay. They can be built up to form areas of pattern.

Beaters Careful beating with a length of wood can alter the form of a completed pot whilst the clay is plastic (129), or texture the surface if used on edge, bound with string, or carved.

Rolling Clay rolled out on a textured surface takes on the texture of that surface (17).

Applied Pieces of clay can be luted on to the surface of the form (131) or simply pressed into place without any slip (137).

Incised Knives and other tools are used to cut into the surface of the clay to produce a design in relief (131).

Sgraffito Lines scratched into the clay surface with a pointed tool (140).

Oxides Oxides or stains mixed into the clay during wedging or rubbed into the surface of the piece tint the clay (82) as well as any glaze subsequently applied (87). They can also be applied by brush, sponge or spray (1) (19) (59).

Slips

Slips are basically a mixture of clay and water, to which other materials may be added to change the colour or texture: their preparation is covered on page 74. Apart from slipware (47), one of the principal uses of slip is that of an underglaze decoration applied to all or part of the surface and affecting the surface colour or texture of the glaze subsequently applied. Whilst clay is the basic raw material in slip, the addition of other materials gives almost limitless possibilities for experiment. Proprietory stains and oxides are the most obvious, but try mixing other materials for test firing under glaze. Keep careful records to enable successful slips to be prepared for general use.

Glazes containing a large proportion of plastic clay can be applied directly to leather-hard clay and fired once directly to glazing temperature: these are known as slip glazes.

Pouring	Slip can be poured over a piece, partially or completely.
Dipping	The pot may be selectively dipped into slip.
Brushing	The slip may be applied with a brush over the entire surface of the pot or as a freely brushed design on a section of it.
Trailing	The decorative possibilities of slipware are briefly covered on pages 38 to 41.
Resists	Resists may be used with slips in exactly the same way as with glazes.
Sgraffito	The coating of slip may be cut away (145) or scratched through to expose the body beneath.
Inlay	Incised or sgraffito designs in the clay body can be filled with slip which, when stiffened, is shaved level with the surrounding surface (16).
Splashing	Slip may be thrown at the pot from a heavily loaded brush or direct from the container to give random designs.

Remember that slips must always be applied before the leather hard state, and each slip in use must be tested for compatibility with the clay body in use. Differences in shrinkage rate will result in the slip breaking away from the body.

Glazes

All glazes, apart from slip glazes, are applied to biscuit ware. The maturing temperature of glaze and body should be more or less the same.

Pouring	Glaze may be poured evenly (23), or deliberately applied in various thicknesses, or in combination with others (33).
Dipping	Selective dipping in a second glaze produces simple, but well-defined designs (33).
Sgraffito	Lines cut through the raw glaze to expose the body beneath: a method which is only successful with a glaze which has no tendency to flow during firing (38).
Resists	Cut paper patterns dampened to the surface of the piece before glaze application are peeled away afterwards, removing the raw glaze attached and revealing the surface beneath (44). Hot wax brushed on to the surface gives a free though less well-defined resist. The raw glaze runs off the wax, which burns away in the firing (44).
Underglaze	Oxides or stains are rubbed, stippled, or brushed on to the surface of the piece before the glaze is applied (20) to alter the known glaze characteristics. Other glazes may be used to form the applied decoration.
Overglaze	Similar techniques can be applied on top of the raw glaze once it has solidified (20) (41).
Enamels	These are painted on to an already-glazed surface and fired at low temperatures. Manufacturer's catalogues give firing temperatures and other directions for use. White glazed wall tiles provide a ready-made base for enamel work.
Transfers	These are bought in from suppliers and used as directed.
Spraying	Spraying gives a very even coating of glaze, but requires specialist equipment and careful precautions to guard against inhalation.

Paint

Artists' colours or household paints may be used to decorate pieces (139) which have been fired to the maturation point of the clay, this being the glazing temperature stipulated by the suppliers.

Glaze application and firing

Application

Bisque ware should be thoroughly brushed to remove fine clay dust which, if left, would prevent the raw glaze from adhering and give rise to crawling or pinholing during firing. Handling should be kept to the minimum, as grease from the hands can cause the same glaze defects.

To coat the inside of a piece, pour in a quantity of glaze which is immediately tipped out as the pot is rotated in the hands (114).

Before glazing the outside, remove any glaze which may have spilled whilst glazing the inside. If the piece is easy to hold by the base it can be plunged into the glaze as far as the finger tips,

assuming that there is sufficient glaze in the bucket. If there is not, the glaze can be poured over the surface as the pot is turned in the hand. Large pots can be laid on two lathes spanning a plastic bowl before the glaze is poured (115). Small pieces, especially those which are difficult to hold, can be plunged completely into the glaze using tongs made from metal rods.

Remember to stir the glaze frequently during a glazing session, and to remove the raw glaze from the base of a pot before it is set aside for packing into the kiln. The distance between the glaze skirt and the base of the pot will depend on how much a particular glaze flows during firing as well as on the form of each piece.

Unlike greenware, raw glazed pieces must not touch each other when packed in the kiln: a gap wide enough to admit the fingers is generally

114 Pouring the glaze from the inside

115 Pouring glaze over the outside

sufficient. Once the raw glazing is completed the packing plan can be prepared and the first pots placed in the kiln. Temperature varies inside the kiln and the bottom corners are sometimes considerably cooler than areas higher up the kiln. It is as well to remember this when packing several pieces which will eventually be brought together and to pack such pieces at the same level; for example a teapot and its lid. Avoid placing any piece close to the sides of the kiln, especially slab pots with large surface areas as these might suffer distortion or variation in glaze finish. Stilts (112) can be used to lift pieces clear of the kiln shelves to prevent adhesion should the glaze run, but these should be used with great care at stoneware temperatures when they may distort the form.

As packing proceeds, space must be allocated directly in line with the spy-hole in the door for temperature cones (111) which are used to control the firing, in conjunction with the pyrometer fitted to electric kilns. The cones are either placed in a special holder (116) or bedded in a thin strip of grogged plastic clay. There is generally a 20° interval between cones adjacent on the coding scale and three are used in the firing. The first indicates that the required temperature is approaching, the second that the final temperature is 20°/30°C away, and the third that the final temperature has been achieved. Each cone bends on reaching its coded temperature.

When packing is complete and the cones placed, the kiln door is closed and padlocked, and the power is switched on a low setting overnight. This first stage dries out the ware completely and warms it through before the controlled temperature rise is begun the following day. This rise should be at the rate of some 100°C per hour with

the kiln bungs in place but less than this as the cone temperatures are approached, indicated by the pyrometer. As the first cone bends, the firing rate should be reduced to allow 20 to 30 minutes to elapse between cone collapses and after the third cone begins to bend the temperature should be held for the same period before the power is switched off. This period of heat soaking ensures an even spread of molten glaze over the surface of the pieces.

116 Cones mounted in special holders and shown in their pre- and post-fired condition

Cooling should be slow initially to avoid damage to the pieces and the kiln door kept closed until the 200°C mark has been passed.

On opening the kiln several glaze faults may be exposed, including crawling (117), pinholing (118) and crazing. Crawling can be produced by an over thick application of raw glaze in addition to the conditions already mentioned. The second can result from fine particles of dust under the raw glaze or from bubbles formed in the glaze at high temperatures during the firing process. The bubbles rise to the surface and burst, the mark left in the molten glaze sometimes failing to heal.

Crazing shows as a network of fine cracks in the glaze, caused by removing a piece from the kiln too quickly or by a basic incompatibility of glaze and clay which leaves the clay in tension and liable to fracture.

Blistering may be caused by bubbling of a thick glaze coating, or the expansion of air pockets trapped in the clay body itself. Often the fault can be traced back to faulty or careless raw glaze application.

There is further shrinkage during firing and the final dimensions will be about seven-eighths of the original in plastic clay.

117 Crawling

118 Pinholing

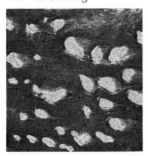 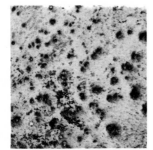

Variations

All the techniques illustrated in the first part of the book can be used to produce pieces in their own right or they can be adapted, refined, developed and combined, as the illustrations in this section suggest. Each caption annotates dimensions, technique, finish and, in some instances, design sources. All are handbuilt from one of three stoneware clays comprising a fine texture for domestic ware, a slightly coarser and darker type for general work, and a grogged clay for some of the sculptural forms. All glazes used are variations on a single basic recipe which have been further varied by ranging the firing temperature between 1200° and 1300°C.

119 *Height 175 mm (6$\frac{7}{8}$ in.)*
Four 'petals' of clay seam jointed around an inflated balloon and coated with a heavily grogged slip dusted with various oxides and stains. Once the clay was self-supporting, the balloon was deflated.
The fired colour is light tan and brown and the form was based on horse-chestnut cases

120 *Height approximately 114 mm (4$\frac{1}{2}$ in.)*
Bowl made from a disc of thin clay formed round loosely bunched polythene, the rim being pinched together to retain the form. The polythene was removed as soon as the clay was self-supporting. Glazed in white with a tan rim

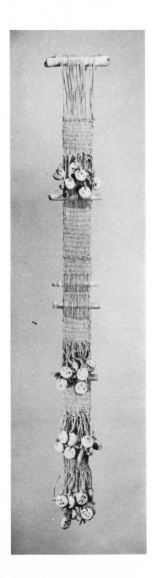

121 Length 1067 mm (42 in.)
   A hanging woven on a simple frame loom
   using twine, driftwood, and tied-on
   bobbles of white-glazed clay. These were
   made from small balls of clay pressed
   between two stamps and pierced for tying

122 Height 203 mm (8 in.)
   White glazed candle holder made from a
   seam jointed core mould. The joint between
   base and top, and the slots in the top, were
   cut into the clay when this was leather hard

123 Heights 140 mm to 216 mm ($5\frac{1}{2}$ in. to $8\frac{1}{2}$ in.)
   Zig-zag forms assembled from clay
   cylinders cut into sections when leather-
   hard. Glazed in white

124 *Height 279 mm (11 in.)*
A bottle built from thick coils cut down to ten facets when leather-hard. Double glazed in white over brown hematite glaze giving a greenish glaze breaking away to rust on edges where thin

125 *Heights 197 mm to 222 mm (7¾ in. to 8¾ in.)*
Cylinders of thin clay, cut, formed, and pinched immediately after removal from the core mould. Glazed in white with red iron oxide stippled on to the pinched edges

126 *Length 787 mm (31 in.)*
A hanging of bluish-green circular tiles knotted together with multiple strands of strong thread. The tiles were cut from sheet clay with a baked bean can and pierced by thin metal tubes, hair grips, (pins) and wire loop modelling tools

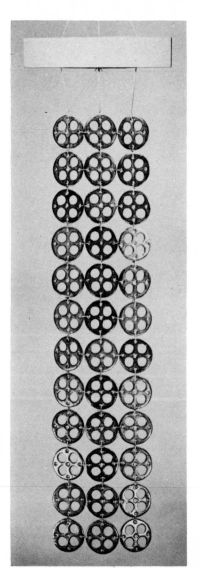

127 Heights 114 mm to 216 mm
(4½ in. to 8½ in.)
Cylinders of clay cut and
formed on removal from the
core mould. Glazed in white
with stippled iron and copper
oxides. Based on studies of
soft plant stems

128 Diameters 83 mm to 114 mm
(3½ in. to 4½ in.)
Assembled from pairs of thumb
pots luted together rim to rim
and pierced by wire loop
modelling tools and wire hair
grips (pins). Glazed in white with
stipplings of one of four oxides,
cobalt, copper, manganese
and iron

129 Height 298 mm (11¾ in.)
An almost spherical coil pot
with its top half beaten to form
four flat faces which were then
indented with a rubber kidney.
Thin coils were added to complete the form which is unglazed
except for the thick white glaze
in the depressions

130 Height 425 mm (16¾ in.)
Coil pot with horizontal pinching between
the coils to join them together and to give a
deeply textured surface. The inside of the
pot is smoothed out completely. Coated
in a white glaze which is broken in parts by
the dark brown body beneath

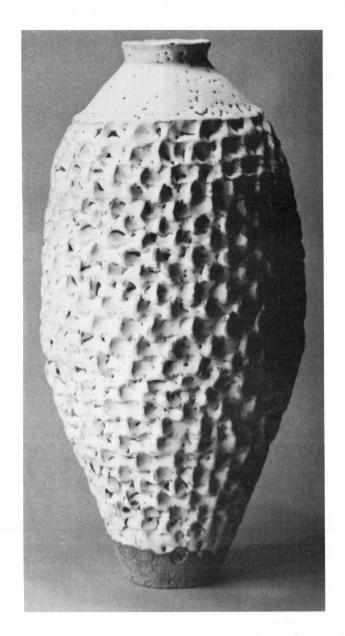

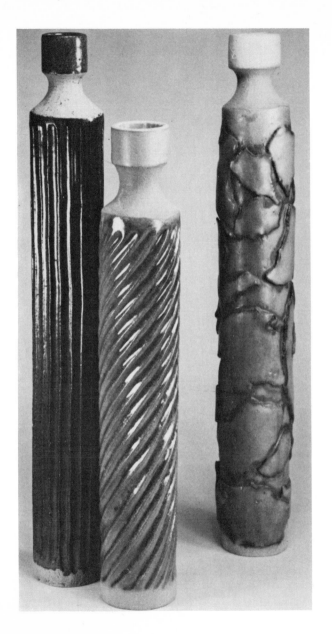

131 Core mould bottles with coiled and slabbed necks; two of them have wire loop modelling tool incisions and the third has torn pieces of thin clay luted into place. All are based on studies of plant stems and tree bark, and are brown, green or grey in colour Heights 387 mm to 457 mm (15$\frac{1}{4}$ in. to 18 in.)

132 Heights 114 mm to 254 mm (4$\frac{1}{2}$ in. to 10 in.)
Jug and mugs made on cardboard core moulds and fitted with pulled handles (98, 99). Glazed in a matt olive green

133 *Diameter across the handles 279 mm (11 in.)*
Casserole assembled from a free standing slab of clay curved on to a cut base, with rims and handles luted into place. The lid is a disc of clay with a carved coil handle. The slightly glassy glaze is light olive in colour

134 *Height of ceramic section 521 mm (20½ in.)*
White glazed, discs, cylinders and knobs threaded on to strands of strong parcel twine to form a free space hanging

135 *Height 127 mm (5 in.)*
Formed from a disc of thin clay draped over the end of a rolling pin and lightly hand crimped. Double glazed in white over purple

136 *Heights 48, 98 and 127 mm (1⅞, 3⅞ and 5 in.)*
White glazed bowl, jug and teapot assembled on core moulds with slabbed spouts and handles

137 *Heights 184 and 286 mm (7¼ and 11¼ in.)*
The taller form has a core mould centre and
the smaller a combination of core mould and
two thumb pots joined rim to rim, to which
small pleated discs of clay were joined.
Glazed in white with hematite and copper
oxide stippling. Based on studies of plant
and marine forms

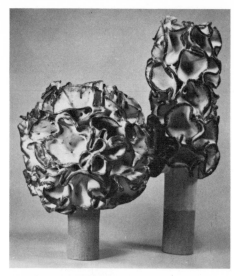

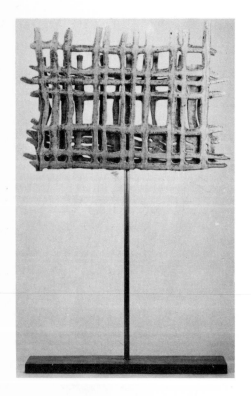

138 Height 419 mm (16½ in.)
(opposite page, below left)
Screen made from a grid of thin coils
flattened together by rolling pin and fired as
two superimposed layers. Unglazed and
mounted on a length of aluminium rod set
into a wooden base

139 Heights 298 mm to 375 mm (11¾ in. to
14¾ in.) (opposite page, below right)
Three forms based on studies of quayside
mooring bollards and coil built on to core
mould bases. After firing they were painted
in brilliant blue and red emulsion paints

140 Heights 108 mm to 127mm (4¼ in. to 5 in.)
Core mould storage jars with a variety of lid
designs and decorations. One is plain
glazed in white, a second is plain glazed in
blue with a press patterned lid, a third has
sgraffito lines cut into the glaze, and the last
sgraffito lines cut into the clay and filled
with brown glaze

141 Height to top of handle 330 mm (13 in.)
Core mould teapot with slabbed top, core
spout and thumb pot lid. Glazed in white

142 *Height 330 mm (13 in.) (below left)*
   Core mould with the top curved and pierced when
   leather-hard. Transparent blue-green glaze.

143 *Height 381mm (15 in.) (below centre)*
   Slabbed form with applied horizontal ribs bounded by
   incised grooves. The curved top was formed on a cardboard
   cylinder. Partly glazed in white. Based on architectural
   studies

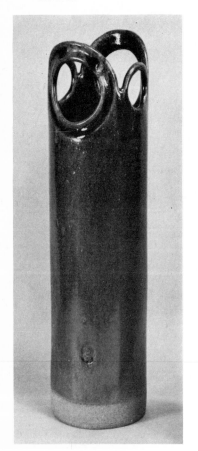

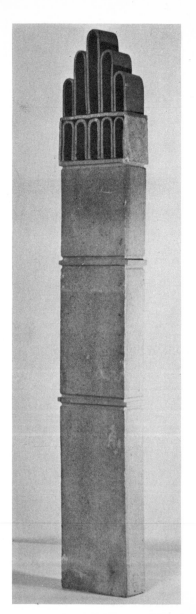

144 *Height 864 mm (34 in.) (opposite page, right)*
Unglazed slab construction based on architectural studies

145 *Height 260 mm (10¼ in.)*
Coil pot thickly coated with black slip through which the plant forms were incised to reveal the clay body. After raw glazing the slipped areas were cleared of glaze before firing to give a dense black design set against a grey glaze. Taken from a fabric design based on Korean pottery forms

146 *Height 305 mm (12 in.)*
Multi-slab form based on architectural studies. Partly glazed in white

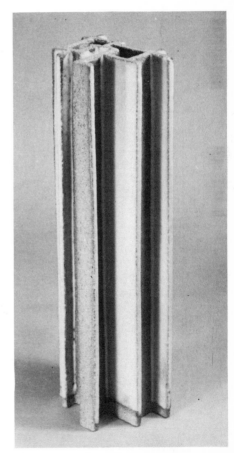

Glossary

BANDING WHEEL Turntable used as a rotating stand for pots during building, finishing or decoration.

BATS Kiln shelves, or, absorbent slabs on which soft clay is spread out to stiffen.

BISCUIT A once-fired piece which is ready for the raw glaze.

BLISTERS Bubbles formed in the glaze and body during firing.

BLOWING Bursting of the body caused by too rapid heating early in the biscuit firing.

BODY The clay from which a pot is made.

CLAY Fine particles of an earthy material which become plastic on the addition of water.

COILING A long established method of pot construction using ropes of clay.

CONES Special ceramic pieces placed in the kiln which, by distortion, indicate a particular temperature.

CRACKLE An intentional and decorative network of cracks in the glaze.

CRAZING A glaze fault similar in appearance to crackle.

CRAWLING Movement of the glaze during firing leaving areas of body exposed.

DIPPING Immersion of a pot in glaze or slip.

DUNTING Cracking or distortion of pots caused by the admission of cold air to the kiln during cooling.

EARTHEN-WARE A porous body, generally fired to 1000–1100°C.

FIRING The heating process which pots undergo in the kiln.

FIT The relationship between glaze and body shrinkage during firing.

FLAKING The breaking away of raw glaze from the body after application.

FOOT The base of a pot.

GLAZE A thin coating of glass fused with the surface of the body during firing.

GLOST The firing of raw glazed pieces.

GREENWARE Unfired pieces.

GROG Fired clay which has been ground down and graded by particle size. One use is to reduce the plasticity of clay to help resist warping.

KNEADING A hand action which mixes plastic clays.

LAWN A sieve used in the preparation of slips and glazes, graded by mesh size.

LEATHER-HARD Clay which has lost its plasticity but is not yet dry. At this stage it is ideal for carving and finishing.

LUTING Jointing of clay pieces with the aid of slip.

PINHOLING Pitting of the glaze during firing, often the result of dust particles lying between the body and the raw glaze.

PLASTICITY The quality which allows damp

	clay to maintain a given form without disintegration or collapse.
PYROMETER	A mechanical device used to measure and indicate kiln temperature.
RAW GLAZE	Glaze as applied to a leather or biscuit pot.
SHIVERING	Flaking of glaze from the surface of a glost-fired piece, caused by an incorrect glaze fit.
SLAKE	The addition of water to dry clay, glaze or slip materials.
SLIP	A sieved mixture of clay and water having a creamy consistency.
SLIP GLAZE	A glaze containing a proportion of plastic clay, usually applied to leather hard greenware.
SLURRY	A rough mixture of clay and water.
SHRINKAGE	The reduction of pot size through drying and firing, usually by approximately one-eighth of the original dimensions.
SINTER	Heating to a point where materials begin to coalesce.
SOAKING	Maintenance of a constant kiln temperature for a period of time at the close of a glost firing.
STILTS	Ceramic supports placed on kiln shelves to carry pots during a glost firing.
STONEWARE	A body fired beyond a point where it ceases to be porous, usually around 1200–1300°C.
TERRACOTTA	A low-fired, unglazed, earthenware body.
VITRIFICA-TION	The fusing of a clay body during firing, so making it non-porous.
WARPING	Distortion of a piece through uneven shrinkage during drying or firing.
WATER	Water of plasticity is the water surrounding the clay particles and giving the clay its plastic qualities: this water is lost in the drying process. Water is also locked chemically in the basic clay material and can only be driven off through heating; the release of this water takes place in the biscuit firing.
WEDGING	A preparatory process by which air is removed from a mass of clay and by which the clay is reduced to an even plasticity suitable for pottery making.

Books

Ball, F. Carlton, and Lovoos, Janice *Making Pottery Without a Wheel* Van Nostrand Reinhold New York

Billington, Dora M. *The Technique of Pottery* B. T. Batsford London

Clark, Kenneth *Practical Pottery and Ceramics* Studio Vista London; Viking Press New York

Colbeck, John *Pottery: The Technique of Throwing* B. T. Batsford London; Watson-Guptill Publications New York

Cooper, Emmanuel *A Handbook of Pottery* Longmans London; St Martin's Press New York

Cowley, David *Working with Clay and Plaster* B. T. Batsford London; Watson-Guptill Publications New York

Green, David *Experimenting with Pottery* Faber and Faber London; Watson-Guptill Publications New York

Green, David *Pottery Materials and Techniques* Faber and Faber London; Watson-Guptill Publications New York

Green, David *Understanding Pottery Glazes* Faber and Faber London; Watson-Guptill Publications New York

Leach, Bernard *A Potter's Book* Faber and Faber London; Transatlantic Arts Inc., Florida

Meyer, Fred *Sculpture in Ceramic* Watson-Guptill Publications New York

Nelson, Glenn C. *Ceramics—A Potter's Handbook* Holt Rinehart and Winston New York

Rhodes, Daniel *Clay and Glazes for the Potter* Sir Isaac Pitman London; Greenberg New York

Rhodes, Daniel *Stoneware and Porcelain* Sir Isaac Pitman London; Pitman Publishing Co. New York

Winterburn, Mollie *The Technique of Handbuilt Pottery* Watson-Guptill Publications New York